This book belongs to a precious and dear one named:

_____
_____

May you always remember that you were made in the image of God, fashioned and formed in your mommy's womb, created by the Lord to do good works - to honor and glorify Him with your life.

You, Precious and Dear One
Published by for His good works publishing, 2025
First Print Edition

Text Copyright ©2025 S. ReNee Ehrhardt-Dilling
Illustrations Copyright ©2025 S. ReNee Ehrhardt-Dilling

Printed in the USA
(IgramSpark)

All rights reserved. No part of this publication may be reproduced, stored in a retrieval system, or transmitted in any form by any means, mechanical, electronic, photocopy, recording, digitally, or otherwise, without the prior permission of the author, except as provided by the United States of America copyright law.

Scripture taken from the New King James Version. Copyright © 1982 by Thomas Nelson, Inc. Used by permission. All rights reserved.

All inquiries should be directed to:
author@forHisgoodworkspublishing.com

ISBN: 979-8-9928425-0-0 Paperback
ISBN: 979-8-9928425-1-7 Hardback
ISBN: 979-8-9928425-2-4 ebook
Library of Congress Control Number: 2025904772

forHisgoodworkspublishing.com

for
His
good
works
publishing

For Junior and Amber,
Thank you both for making me Mimi to Lili and
for allowing Papaw and me to
have a part in her first
two years. Because of her,
this book exists.

Years ago, even before you and I were born, God created the heavens and the universe.

Yes, this same **God** who created the earth...

Is the **very same** God Who created you in your mommy's womb.

For You,
Oh Precious One...
you were
created in the
image of
God.

Make no mistake, Dear One,
YOU are NO mistake.

Yes, before you were born. He knit you together in your **mommy's womb**. He fashioned and formed you.

Yes, He even chose for you to be a boy or a girl.

He even chose **when** you would be born.

He even chose **where** you would be born.

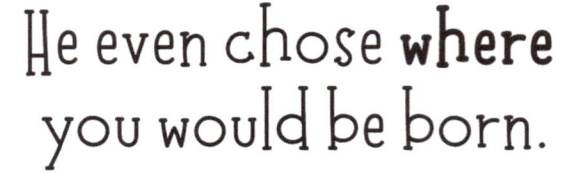

He even chose **your nationality**.

He knows the **exact number of hairs** on your head.

He knows the **exact number** of days of your life.

He knows what makes you cry.

He knows what **makes you** happy.

He knows **every word you will ever say**, even before you say it! He even knows **your thoughts** before you think them!

That is pretty amazing, isn't it?

**Yes,
He knows
EVERYTHING
about you!**

You can't ever surprise Him with anything you do or don't do.

You **can't ever hide** from Him,
because He **sees you** all the time.

Remember, Precious and Dear One, He created you for a purpose.

He **wants you** to live your life to honor and glorify Him.

A NOTE FROM THE AUTHOR:

Thank you for reading this book! If you haven't already, then one day soon, I hope you realize that this God Who made you, wants you to put all your trust in Him because He wants you to spend eternity (forever and ever) in Heaven with Him.

He never changes. He never sleeps. He never tells a lie. He is a holy God and wants you to know Him. He wants you to love Him with all your heart, mind, and soul.

You can know Him through Jesus Christ. Jesus came to earth to live a perfect life for an imperfect people, like you and me.

You see, God is Holy. That means He can't have sin in His Kingdom. We can't do anything on our own to earn our way to be with Him in eternity.

Jesus came and paid the price that we owe for the sin and all the bad that we do. He not only died for our sins, but He rose again and is alive. God sent His Holy Spirit to stay with us and to help us. Because of His Holy Spirit, we never have to be alone.

He doesn't just want you to live in eternity with Him. He wants to live through you now as you live each day. He wants you to live your life to please and honor Him.

Remember, You, Precious One, were made for a purpose. It is my prayer that you learn to trust in the Lord and that you believe His Word, the Bible. His Word is true and you can believe all His promises and you can trust what you read in the Bible!

If you realize your need for Jesus and His salvation, tell Him. Agree with Him that you have sinned and offended Him. Ask Him to help you live your life to please and honor Him. Knowing Jesus as your Savior doesn't mean you will live a pain-free life or even an easy life, but you will never have to be alone. You will always have His Holy Spirit in you and with you always. Blessings to you!

Be sure to check out the following Scriptures in God's Word for the truths shared in this book. Genesis 1:1; 1:16-18; 1:26-27. Deuteronomy 6:5. Job 14:5-7; Psalm 90:1-2,10,12; Psalm 139:1-18. Proverbs 16:4. Jeremiah 23:24. Matthew 10:30; Acts 17:26-28; Galatians 1:5; 1 Corinthians 6:19-20; Hebrews 4:13-15; Revelation 4:11.

Jesus said, "I am the way, the truth, an the life. No one comes to the Father except through Me"
(John 14.6, NKJV).

Jesus also said, "And this is eternal life, that they may know You, the only true God, and Jesus Christ whom You have sent"
(John 17.3, NKJV).

"The grass withers, the flower fades,
But the word of our God stands forever"
(Isaiah 40.8, NKJV).

Scan the QR code to go directly to our website:

To contact the author, you can send snail mail at
Post Office Box 431
Ehrhardt, SC 29081
United States of America

You can also contact the author at author@forHisgoodworkspublishing.com

About the author:
ReNee believes as the Bible teaches that everyone of us is made in the image of God and we are each meant to live our lives to glorify and honor the Lord. She also considers it a privilege to have been able to work with so many children most of her life through children's ministries, as a missionary in Mexico and as a public school teacher.
She wants for all children to know just how special they are to the Lord and that they are each created to glorify Him with their lives.
ReNee lives with her one and only favorite hubby, Chad in Ehrhardt, SC. She has two adult stepchildren, Junior (Amber) and Ginny. She is Mimi to Lili and Amon.

A sketch of the author with her hubby and granddaughter, Lili

Interested in purchasing multiple copies for a group,
school, or organization?
Contact me at:
author@forHisgoodworkspublishing.com

Be sure to check out forHisgoodworkspublishing.com for more books. This book is also available in ebook format.
This book will be offered in multiple languages, soon!

Special thanks to Faith for your illustrations.
You did a fabulous job!

www.ingramcontent.com/pod-product-compliance
Lightning Source LLC
Chambersburg PA
CBHW061157030426
42337CB00002B/32